3AM QUESTIONS

Annika M. Zimmermann

For Emily.

Bibliographic information on the German National Library: The German National Library lists this publication in the German National Library; detailed bibliographic data is available on the internet at dnb.dnb.de.

© 2021 Annika M. Zimmermann

Manufacturing and publication: BoD – Books on Demand, Norderstedt

ISBN: 9783753482736

Important note:

This book covers sensitive topics. The following questions are of a very personal nature and can have different effects on people. They should, however, not have a negative influence on your mental state, psyche and actions.

Table of Contents

Foreword	9
Chapter 1: Identity	11
Chapter 2: Relationships	83
Chapter 3: Sadness	163
Chapter 4: Life	225
Chapter 5: Success	291
Acknowledgements	353

Foreword

People ask themselves questions every day. Many of them don't get answered. Many of them never will be. Some of the questions may be so difficult or complex that they seem not to have an answer. They get asked over and over again but nobody ever knows how to respond. And how could they?

There are also some questions that people just don't want to answer. They might make them feel very uncomfortable or remind them of situations or feelings they would rather forget, so they avoid saying anything. But above all, most of our questions remain unanswered because we never say them out loud.

I do that…and each day more and more questions come to mind. Some of these questions are my constant companions and have been for years now. Every now and then I feel like I've finally found a response until it slips away and changes its appearance, just like I have changed mine throughout the years. The responses to these questions also change with my values, my attitude, and my mindset as life goes on. The fact remains, I haven't and never will have a definite answer to all of them… and that can be very overwhelming. I guess I'll just have to make peace with the fact that I might never have the answers to all of my questions.

However, I still feel that thinking about them and dealing with them is what's important. Whether you discuss them with someone you trust or lay awake thinking about them at 3am – the key is to find a way to deal with these questions and not be discouraged if you can't find the answer straight away. That's why I decided to write them down.

In this book, I want to share some of the big questions I've asked myself at one point or another with you – 333 of them, to be exact. They revolve around the thoughts that keep my mind busy. Some of them I've asked myself, some of them I've asked others and many of them are meant to be asked unto others but I haven't gotten around to asking out loud yet. Some of them have been very meaningful to me, some of them still are, and some of them have had an impact on the people around me. However, they are all there. And now, they are here for you to read. You will enter my personal thoughts. Maybe you can relate to some of them. Maybe, they'll inspire you. Maybe they'll be the foundation for long conversations. Maybe they'll help you or maybe, you won't feel so alone anymore when it comes to certain situations.

Either way, I hope you can take something away from this book that will help you along in life or even just in this moment – whatever that may be.

Chapter 1: Identity

What makes you you?

What happens
if your heart tells you one thing
but your head tells you another?

Do you control your thoughts
or do your thoughts control you?

Why are the promises you make to yourself
always the hardest to keep?

Have you ever had to make a choice
that broke your heart
but healed your soul?

Are you really happy

or just pretending to be?

When should you stop putting others first?

Does anyone ever genuinly know
what they're doing?

What memory makes you very sad
but also very happy at the same time?

Would your younger self be proud
of who you have become?

When do you feel happiest
in your own skin?

What is the most important lesson
you have learned in your life so far?

Who am I, really?

How often have you said *yes*
to something
you'd rather have said *no* to?

Is being able to keep secrets
a good or a bad thing?

What do you lose yourself in?

Do you ever wish you could feel the way you did
at a certain point in your past
just one more time?

How am I supposed to deal with all of this
if I can't even deal with myself?

Am I holding onto something
I actually need to let go of?

What is something *only you* can do?

If your life were to flash before your eyes,
would it be worth watching?

What do you want to be remembered for?

Have you already found yourself

or are you still looking?

Am I forcing myself
to become someone
I'm not?

I've always wondered:
how different are the versions of me
that live within the minds of others?

Are you *truly* listening?

Why don't you understand that you are worth more than being a second choice?

Have you done something good
for yourself today?

What's something
that means a lot to you
but no one quite understands?

Have you ever been
afraid of yourself?

What if I'm not
the person I thought I was?

Do you ever get tired of being nice?

Instead of forgiving others all the time,
have you ever considered maybe
forgiving yourself?

Why is there always so much going on
in my head?

Could it be, you're not as strong as you're pretending to be?

What do you think about before you go to sleep at night and what's the first thing that comes to mind when you wake up in the morning?

If you had the chance to erase
one specific memory from your brain,
which one would it be?

Are you okay?

When was the last time
you treated yourself?

How is the public version of you different
from the private version of you?

Why me?

Am I doing anything
about the things
that bother me?

Isn't being alone with yourself
the best feeling sometimes?

What is it you like most about yourself?

How much happier would you be
if you would just stop overthinking
every little thing in your life?

Are you where you need to be?

Time is precious.
So, dare to ask yourself:
who is *really* worthy of your time?

Isn't it easy to lose yourself?

But what if you didn't even need to fall in love
because you loved yourself so much
that it would be enough?

Why do you keep looking for answers
in other people?

Are you aware that there are people
who couldn't live without you?

Maybe, just maybe…

                do you deserve better?

If a camera can't capture the beauty of the night sky,
how could it ever be able to capture
the beauty of you?

Have you done anything
worth remembering yet?

Do you feel the need to control everything
or are you able to trust
that things will work themselves out?

What would it be like
to meet yourself?

Have you ever tried to spend some time
alone with yourself?
No phone, no books, no music...
nothing to do, just you alone with your thoughts?

Are you healed or just distracted?

Have you started taking care of yourself
or are we still working on that?

Why are you apologizing for every little thing
as if you were the one to blame?

Who could know us better
than we know ourselves?

Am
I
thinking
too
much
again?

Have you ever tried to look at yourself
the way you look at other people?
Are you as harsh on others
as you are on yourself?

You know you can't force people to see your worth, don't you?

But honestly… Why do you care?

How am I supposed to explain
what's going on in my head
when I don't even understand it myself?

Am I a good person?

How is it I am so great at giving advice
but so bad at taking it?

Are you still you
if you see yourself a certain way
but everyone else sees you differently?

If we can lose ourselves, don't you think
we can also find ourselves again?

Chapter 2: Relationships

Why is it, no matter how much time we spend together, it's never enough?

Isn't it crazy how you could have a million options
but you would always choose
this one person?

Do I miss you
or do I miss the way you made me feel?

Why are we always quietest around the people
we've got the most to say to?

Can a game of lies ever be won?

Is it possible that we have to fall apart
in order to realize how much we need to fall
back together again?

The person you used to talk to all day –

where are they now?

Why is it so hard to hate you?

Have you ever had someone hurt you so bad
but you still couldn't stop loving them?

Do you still keep secrets for people who have turned their back on you?

Why do I feel like
the more I need you
the less you need me?

When did you turn into somebody else?

Isn't it funny, how we sometimes settle for
the bare minimum when there are people out there
who want to give us the world?

Have you ever had to choose between two people
and then ended up losing both?

What do you think of

 when you hear my name?

Why is it that every time
someone tells me they'll never leave,
that's exactly what they do?

Is it wrong that I still have hope for you?

Have you really moved on or are you still just trying to convince yourself that you have?

Do you know that feeling you get
when you expect so much from someone
just because you'd do so much for them?

Can you get over someone
without losing them?

Isn't it funny how someone
could be on your mind every day
and they could never know?

Doesn't the answer lie in how they treat you?

What do you *really* think of them?

Why should they like you
if you don't even like yourself?

Can you please tell me how to talk to you?

When did late night texts turn into *"k bye"*?
When did *"I miss you"* turn into *"I'm busy rn"*?
When did *"I love you"* turn into *"did you ever love me"*?

What if I'm just scared to see you
with someone else?

Did we really go through all this
just to become strangers again?

Have you ever thought about the first time
you met someone and compare it
to where you guys are now?

What are they doing when they're not here?

Do you want to stay up until 5am and watch
the stars with me?
Do you want to hold my hand while I'm sitting
in the passenger seat?
Do you want to sleep in my arms and dance to our
favorite songs and kiss in the rain?
Do you?

Will we ever be able to talk
the way we used to talk?

Is it me you think about at night?

Did they really leave you for the better
or did they just leave because
they didn't need you anymore?

We played the game of love,
over and over again,
and guess who won?

Why do I still look for you in everyone else?

If they died tomorrow,
would you regret the things you said?
Or maybe the things you didn't say?

Will you want me more
if I act like I want you less?

Do you ever wish you'd receive
as much love as you give?

Have you ever fallen in love
with the idea of a person
instead of the actual person?

Can
you
please
stay
forever?

Isn't it weird how we keep making excuses
for people who keep showing us
exactly who they are?

Do you think of me
the same way I think of you?

Is there anything more painful than
watching the one you want
want someone else?

How long have you been playing
this game with me?

Do you ever wish you could just
hug that one specific person
just one more time?

Isn't no answer still an answer?

Even though we love each other,
could it be possible that we're just
not right for each other?

Can someone love
more than one person at once?

Have you ever considered that
losing someone could make you
find yourself?

How is everything about you so perfect?

Did you actually forgive them
or did you just pretend to
because you still want them in your life?

Are you really busy
or do you just
forget about me sometimes?

Have you ever said *"goodbye"*
just to hear *"don't go"*?

Do you even know
how much you mean to me?

Can you please look into my eyes
and just tell me the truth?

Do you remember the first time you saw them smile?
Their first touch? Their first words to you
and your heart going crazy in your chest
while you just looked at them?

Will you take my hand
and go down this road with me?

You know you shouldn't beg
for a relationship with anyone,
right?

Do you ever miss someone
but then remind yourself
why they aren't in your life anymore?

So, you noticed the attitude
but not how you caused it?

You can delete my number,
our pictures and dates,
but how are you going to
delete the memories?

If they truly cared,
wouldn't they want to show you?

Can you promise me
not to make any promises?

Isn't it the worst thing ever
when you want to tell someone
something you really want them to know
but you're not close enough anymore
so it would be weird?

Have you ever caught yourself
staring at someone and smiling,
you're so in love with them?

Do you really think
you have to let them back into your life
just because that's what they want?

Can you imagine forever with them?

When was the moment
you knew you've fallen for them?

Did you ever think you were over someone
but then, when you see them again,
you feel your heart shatter
in your chest?

Why do you keep letting them
play games with you?

Do they know about your craziest stories
or have they lived them with you?

How much more one-sidedness can I take?

Have you ever had to say a goodbye
without knowing that it would be
the last?

Will you ever not want them in your life?

What's worse,
having to leave someone you love
or to be left by someone you love?

Would you rather give them up
or give up yourself?

Pinky promise?

Chapter 3: Sadness

How are there so many people in this world
and yet I still feel so alone?

Can you remember
how many times you said you were fine
when you really weren't?

Do you ever just feel... *stuck*?

What if we could talk to those we've lost
one more time?

Why does every day feel the same?

I am doing so god damn much…

So why do I still feel like
it's not enough?

Do I have the right
to feel what I am feeling?

Why does it make perfect sense in my head
but as soon as I say it out loud,
it doesn't?

Isn't it tiring,
always having to function?

Do you ever feel like everything is fine
but at the same time nothing is?

How do you help someone
who doesn't want to be helped?

If good things take time,
why does it feel like our time
is already up?

Even though I am shouting at the top of my lungs –

why don't you hear me?

How did I end up here?

Why is it so hard
to put feelings into words?

What is the kindest thing I can do for myself
whenever I am feeling like this?

What the hell is wrong with me?

Isn't it cruel how the person who
tries to keep everyone happy
often ends up the loneliest?

Can broken things still be beautiful?

Why do I constantly feel like everyone hates me
and everything is my fault?

When
will
this
stop?

Do you remember the time
when everything was so much easier?

Have you ever been lying in bed
and had to cry so hard,
you had to cover your mouth
to not make a sound?

Am I going insane?

How do I always get myself
into situations
I then can't get out of?

Can't you see how much I'm hurting?

What if there is no right way?

If everything happens for a reason,
can someone explain
why this is happening?

Where is this anger coming from?

Don't you agree that
this is a kind of pain
you shouldn't
have to feel?

Why do you never pick up the phone
when I need you to?

Can anyone tell me
what I'm doing wrong?

They say, in the end
they always come back...

so why didn't they?

Why is it
that nothing ever changes,
no matter how hard I try?

Do you ever accept feeling bad about something rather than just talking to someone about it because you feel like you'd annoy them?

Am I the reason
all these things
keep happening to me?

Will it *ever* be easy?

How would I feel now
if I had gotten to say
everything I wanted to say?

Why do you keep lying to yourself?

Without darkness,
how would we be able
to see the stars?

How often have you had to move on
from something that wasn't your fault
without ever getting an apology?

Do you ever look at old
pictures or videos and see
how good life used to be?

Can you please come back?

Do you ever feel stupid
about your own thoughts?

How do you expect sad music
to help you get out of a sad mood?

Isn't it okay
to feel a lot of feelings?

Doesn't *"being alive"*
mean so much more
than just surviving?

Would we still know
what happiness feels like
if we were never sad?

Do you sometimes struggle
to do even the easiest tasks?

Have you ever avoided the mirror
because you just couldn't stand
looking at yourself?

Why would you reopen healing wounds?

Is being alone
        and being lonely
                the same thing?

Why is it always me
who puts in all the fucking effort?

Can you please hug me
and tell me
everything will be okay?

What if instead of being sad it's over,
we were to appreciate that it happened
and take what we can from it?

How many times
can the same thing
break your heart?

What keeps us going
when we're at our lowest?

Do you ever feel really happy
but also really sad
at the same time?

Don't we all struggle sometimes?

What if all the bad things
that are happening to you right now
are the reason you'll achieve
infinite happiness one day?

Chapter 4: Life

Are you more afraid of change
or of things staying the same?

Why is there always so little time
for the things that make us
feel alive?

Is it really worth
holding onto something,
if it means losing yourself in the process?

What do you think
your dreams are trying to tell you?

Why do our hearts need so much more time
to accept what our minds already know?

Is there any way around
growing up?

What's your biggest reason
to wake up tomorrow?

Have you ever watched a car drive by
or looked into a house through a window and imagined
what the people inside might be doing?
What their life is like? What their conversations are about
and what their goals and apirations are?
What are their stories?

What if a day had 48 hours?

Isn't it weird that
we can feel other people's looks
on our skin?

Why is it, the older you get

                    the shorter a year feels?

How many mistakes can you make
until there is no going back?

Why do we stop doing things that we love
just because people tell us
we're *"too old"*?

Can you really plan your future?

When you think about the size of the universe, does it ever scare you

how small we actually are?

What is the difference
between living and existing?

Have you noticed how people change
when they don't get what they want
from you?

What if all you have to do
is give it
just a little more time?

Isn't it weird, leaving school
and suddenly having to do things
without anyone telling you how?

Does the "perfect time"
to do something
even exist?

Why should you spend
more than five minutes
worrying about something
that won't matter
in five years time?

What are little things you love?

What would be something that you'd look forward to telling your grandchildren about?

Is life really hard?
Or do we make it hard for ourselves?

How do you play a game
with no rules?

We choose what we surround ourselves with
based on looks, but what happens
when those looks fade?

What would our planet look like,
if humans had never existed?

Remember how you were able
to keep yourself entertained for hours
with nothing more than a few plastic figurines
and your imagination?

Is it worth it?

Do you ever want to leave everything behind
and just move somewhere
far far away?

What gives anyone the right
to interfere in *your* life?

Isn't it funny
how the smallest things
can have the biggest impact?

How do you escape reality?

Have you ever had
to keep something to yourself,
knowing you can *never* talk
to anyone about it?

What makes a place a home?

Do you ever look at the birds and wonder
what their freedom must feel like?

We won't be here forever.
Don't you think you should shoot your shot?
After all, don't you miss all the shots you don't take?

Is there any sight more beautiful
than an orange glowing sunset
with pink cotton candy clouds?

How bad can it get?

Where would you like to be
in this exact moment?

Why should I regret anything
if there are both good and bad lessons
to learn in life?

To what degree can you
actually have control of the
course of your life?

What if all of this isn't real?

Isn't it the worst feeling ever
when you really want to change something
about a certain thing, but it just isn't
in your power to do it?

Do you remember
the carefree lightheartedness
we had when we were children?
What made it go away?

When is it acceptable
to break the law?

Isn't it cruel
how the most difficult decisions
are often the most important ones?

What is life asking of me?

If we get too caught up in the past,
don't we miss everything great that
is happening in the present,
right in front of our eyes?

Is it a bad thing
that I just need a break
every now and then?

Do you even know
how much you don't know?

Money? *Sex?*

Memories?

Relationships?

Fun?

What is life really about?

Family? *Peace?*

Faith?

Success?

Experiences?

Why does life happen so fast?

Isn't it scary how vulnerable we are –
simply made of meat, blood and bones?

How did I get so caught up in this?

What are the things you would regret
if you didn't do them?

Will a certain level of consciousness
still exist after I die?

If you could choose to start over,

would you?

Why do we only recognize the "good times" when we are no longer in them?

Is it possible to have everything
and nothing at the same time?

What if our dreams were actually a part of reality
but we deem them so weird and messed up
that we retreat to what we
now call *"reality"*?

Why do people keep getting involved
in things that don't involve them?

Do you know those moments
when life just doesn't feel real?

Is
now
the
time
to
let
go?

Aren't the best things in life
always the things that we
haven't planned?

Chapter 5: Success

When you close your eyes,
do you see darkness or
do you paint pictures?

Why are you doing this?

How far would you go to go far?

Have you ever thought
"I'll never be able to do this",
but then you went and did it anyway?

Is failing worse than never trying?

What if today's pain

                is tomorrow's power?

Why am I so afraid
to give up the things
I know won't take me
where I want to go?

Can perfectionsism
kill perfection?

Isn't it funny
how one day we just drop people
we once swore we couldn't live without?

What do you want *most* in life?

Why do I keep talking myself out of things
I am excited about?

Are you afraid of the storm?

How do you expect to get better
in the same environment
that made you sick?

Am I using my time wisely?

Based off the way you work –
If you had a company, would you
hire yourself?

When did you stop
chasing your dreams?

All these expectations…

Do other people put them on you
or do you put them on yourself?

Where do I want to be
five years from now?

Instead of worrying about the future all the time,
have you ever taken a moment to stop
and look back on how far you've
already come?

Do you think I could touch the stars
if I just stretch far enough?

Is there anything worse than
not being taken seriously?

When did you last push the boundaries
of your comfort zone?

Have you ever had a really great idea you were
really passionate about but then one day
watched it die right in front of you?

Is it really failing

or is it learning?

Should I just keep pretending
until I actually get there one day?

Why
do
I
always
want
more?

I have all these dreams
and ambitions,
so why do I still keep
wasting my time?

Will I ever have this chance again?

If you want something,
why don't you just go ahead
and get it?

What is one thing
other people admire you for?

Are you doing this
to make yourself happy...

...or are you doing it
for someone else?

Have you drank enough water today?

Can you even begin to imagine
what you are capable of?

How do I know
which path to choose?

If you had to write a book about your life,
could you fill all the pages?

What do you have to lose?

Why is it so hard to keep in mind
that life's not a race
and I can do things in my own time?

How is it I never doubt anyone

                                              but myself?

Have you noticed that
we can't achieve happiness
through other people,
only through ourselves?

Are you surrounding yourself with
things, people and situations
that are good for you?

Where does this
constant restlessness
come from?

They say count your blessings –
but with so many blessings,
can I even count them all?

I'm sorry,
but what is so wrong
about doing it my way?

How am I supposed to figure out what I want
when I want something different every day?

Now, tell me –

what are you so afraid of?

Why are you trying to impress people
you don't even care about?

Are you here because you *want* to be
or because you feel like you *have* to be?

What is one thing you would do
if you weren't so afraid?

Once again I ask myself...

Why do I keep allowing people to waste my time?

What's stopping you from being your own biggest role model?

Would we be afraid of falling
if we knew
we wouldn't hit the ground?

Are you putting your energy
into the right things?

How can you ever know
if you never try?

What if the doors that closed on
us weren't missed chances but
convenient coincidences that
stopped us from entering
the wrong room?

Maybe the time has come
to start acting like the person
I want to be?

To those who told me I'd lose in life...
What does it feel like to see me succeed?

How boring must their life be
for them to care so damn much
about yours?

Do you ever wonder where you would be today
if you had simply made one small
different decision?

Why are you so scared to try again?

What can I do **right now**
to get one step closer
to where I want to be?

Acknowledgements

This book wouldn't be what it is without the major support from certain people in my life. First off, I would like to thank my editor, Megan Bowen, who sacrificed her valuable time to help turn this book into the best version of itself that it could possibly be. Thank you so much for supporting my ideas and your willingness to help wherever you can. I would also like to thank Kaye Jorga for the wonderful cover design and Frank Jorga for having so much patience with me. This is only the beginning, I promise. Great things are coming.

I also want to thank Julia Schoch, who is a very special person in my life. I appreciate the fact that you are someone I can always count on to be interested in my projects and I can always rely on your honest opinion.

Last but not least, a big thank you goes out to my dear friend Emily Rehak, who has been my number one supporter whilst writing this book. Thank you for being even more excited about my projects than I am. Thank you for discussing my ideas with me for hours. Thank you for all the thoughts, love and support you have put into this idea and thank you for pushing me to always do my best. You are a true blessing in my life.

Most of all, I owe the biggest thank you to you!
Thank you for reading or even just skimming through my book. It's a very personal thing for me to share these thoughts but I know there are probably a lot of people who feel the same, who have the same thoughts and ask themselves the same questions I do.

I hope this helps someone feel less alone and no longer like they're the only one who has had these thoughts. I hope this inspired you and gave you something to think about. I hope someone will use these questions to start meaningful conversations with others. I hope someone has gotten to know themselves a little bit better while reading this. Even if all you got from this book was a perfect Instagram quote. I hope that seeing these questions in my book help you with your own 3am thoughts.
I hope you've enjoyed reading this and most of all, I hope you'll choose a path that is good for you.

Always remember.
You are enough.

<3

CPSIA information can be obtained
at www.ICGtesting.com
Printed in the USA
FSHW020951220621
82587FS